Series 601

A LADYBIRD 'ACHIEVEMENTS' BOOK

UNDERWATER EXPLORATION

by
RICHARD BOWOOD

with illustrations by
B. KNIGHT

Publishers: Wills & Hepworth Ltd., Loughborough

First published 1967   ©   *Printed in England*

The World beneath the Sea

Man has explored and mapped the dry land; he has climbed the highest mountains, penetrated the densest jungles and crossed the most desolate deserts. All these are measured and known, but the exploration of the vast world beneath the sea has only just begun.

Nearly three-quarters of the earth's surface is water to an average depth of two and three-quarter miles. The immense area of the ocean bed with its great level plains, its sunken mountain ranges and its deep canyons still awaits the explorers.

The seas teem with animal and plant life. There are more than twenty thousand species of fish of every shape, size and colour. The largest sea creature is the whale, and a blue whale can weigh a hundred tons. The smallest are so tiny that they can only be seen through a microscope, yet they are of dreamlike beauty. Between these two extremes is a great range of creatures; fish, crustaceans such as lobsters and crabs, and such molluscs as the giant squid and the oyster and cockle.

Underwater plants have an infinite variety, too; there are many kinds of seaweed, and countless strange plants. There are even some sea creatures which look like plants.

In the eternal darkness of the deep, live animals and plants which man has not yet seen. This book describes man's exploration and achievements in this strange world of the sea.

4   *The strange world of the sea*

7214 0140 6

Divers of Ancient Days

Modern science has made it possible for man to descend safely to considerable depths, and to stay underwater for a long time. He can wear a diving suit with an air-tube to the surface, or he can carry his air supply strapped to his back with a tube to his mouth. He can go down in a submarine or in a specially constructed observation chamber.

But when a man dives without any equipment he can only stay under as long as he can hold his breath, and the depth to which he can go with safety is limited by the weight of the water above him, which exerts a considerable pressure on the body. At thirty feet this pressure is thirteen pounds per square inch, at one hundred feet it is forty-five pounds per square inch, and at one hundred and fifty feet it becomes sixty-six pounds.

Men have dived for thousands of years, but stayed under only for short periods. Xerxes, King of Persia employed a famous Greek diver in 460 B.C. to dive to salvage treasure from sunken ships. Alexander the Great used divers at the siege of Tyre in 333 B.C. to destroy the booms put up by the enemy to defend the city from his ships.

Divers were used in ancient days to collect coral, mother-of-pearl and sponges from the bed of the Mediterranean. Sponges are still obtained by divers who plunge from boats, holding a heavy stone fastened to a rope. The weight takes them quickly to the bottom, where they cut the sponges with a knife, put them in a bag, tug the rope as a signal and are hauled to the surface.

Xerxes, King of Persia, sees a gold breastplate brought up by Scyllis—a famous diver—in 460 B.C.

Pearl Diving

One of the most beautiful and precious gems is the pearl, which is found at the bottom of the sea. A pearl is a growth inside the shell of a pearl-oyster. Oysters line their shells with a very smooth substance called mother-of-pearl, and if anything gets inside a shell the oyster makes that smooth too. If, for example, a grain of sand gets in the shell, the oyster covers it with layers of mother-of-pearl, until it becomes perfectly smooth—and that is the pearl.

About a thousand oysters have to be collected to find one shell containing a pearl, and it is only occasionally that a perfect pearl of great value is found.

The richest pearl-oyster beds are off Ceylon, in the Persian Gulf and in the southern Pacific Islands. Pearls are also found off Australia and the coast of California.

Pearl divers learn to hold their breath for a long time, a minute and a half or even two minutes. They also train their bodies to withstand the pressure of the water at depths of seventy-five feet or more.

As with sponge divers, a weighted line is lowered to the bottom of the sea from a boat and the diver plunges to collect as many oysters as he can into a string bag. Then he guides himself up with the weighted line, or is hauled up to the boat.

Pearl divers at work

The Diving Helmet

The most obvious difficulty in diving is the fact that a man can only hold his breath for a short time. Skilled pearl divers can only manage a minute and a half, or sometimes, two minutes. To stay longer under water a man must have a supply of air, and one way is to use a pipe from his mouth to the surface.

For several centuries, men have tried to devise a method of breathing under water with an air-pipe. About the year 1500 the great Italian artist and inventor, Leonardo da Vinci, drew designs for diving equipment with air-pipes. Many other people worked on the same idea, but none of the inventions were really practicable.

The first really efficient diving helmet was invented in 1819 by Augustus Siebe. Siebe was a Prussian who had fought at the Battle of Waterloo with Wellington against Napoleon. He settled in England and founded the great firm of diving engineers, Siebe, Gorman & Company Limited.

Siebe's first diving helmet was fixed to the diver's jacket. Air was pumped down a pipe to the helmet and the pressure of the air kept the water out. It escaped freely at the diver's waist, and for this reason it was known as the 'open' helmet.

This helmet was successfully used for sixteen years, until it was replaced by Siebe's 'closed' diving helmet. The 'open' helmet had the disadvantage that the diver had to move carefully, for if he bent down carelessly his jacket might fill with water and drown him.

An early 'open' diving helmet

The First Submarines

Just as men tried for hundreds of years to invent diving helmets and suits, so inventors worked on designs for underwater vessels. The first successful submarine was built in London in 1620 by a Dutchman, Cornelius van Drebble. It had a wooden hull protected on the outside by greased leather, and was propelled by twelve oars with watertight joints. The boat made many trips down the Thames from London, but could only submerge a few feet.

A more effective submarine was built by an American, David Bushnell, in 1776, during the American War of Independence. She was called *Turtle*, and was built of wood, rather like an egg, and was driven by a hand-turned screw. She was a one-man submarine with a number of novel devices. She submerged effectively but was unsuccessful in trying to blow up British men-of-war at anchor.

Another American, Robert Fulton, built a submarine in 1801 which carried a crew of three, one in command and two to turn a propeller by hand. She was called *Nautilus*, the same as the first atomic submarine built a hundred and fifty years later. Fulton's Nautilus could dive to twenty-five feet. On the surface she used a strange sail which folded up, like an umbrella, when the ship dived. She behaved well on her trials but neither the French, British nor American governments would take the idea of a submarine seriously.

Other inventors added their ideas as the years passed, and gradually the submarine came into being as an effective kind of warship.

Fulton's Nautilus—one of the first submarines

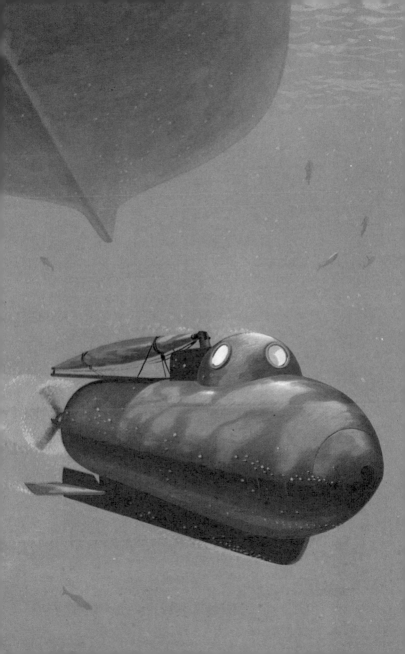

The Wreck of the Royal George

The *Royal George*, a large man-of-war, sank at Spithead in 1782 and lay upright in sixty-five feet of water. As well as being a great disaster the wreck was a danger to shipping in that busy anchorage. Attempts were made to raise her by passing hawsers under the hull to two ships, but with no success, and the great ship lay rotting on the sea-bed for fifty-seven years.

It was in 1839 that the problem of demolishing the wreck was undertaken by soldiers of the Royal Engineers. A Colonel, four other officers and thirty-two sappers were given the task, and their work was of the greatest importance, for it laid the foundations of all subsequent deep-sea diving and salvage operations. Equipment has been improved, but the methods worked out for the first time in the salvage of the *Royal George* established future procedures.

The soldiers were enterprising, intelligent and brave, and they found out for themselves how to solve the problems which faced them and contrived and used new equipment.

The most important part of the new equipment was Siebe's 'closed' diving helmet, which was an important improvement on his 'open' helmet. The new type was sealed to a water-tight diving suit, which could be inflated by the air pump to counteract the pressure of the water on the diver. Moreover, the new type of helmet enabled the diver to move more freely and to bend down without danger of flooding the helmet.

The Royal George just after she sank in 1782

Demolition of the Royal George

When the Royal Engineers began work on the wreck of the Royal George in 1839, their tasks were to salvage the cannons, timbers, brass and anything of value and then to demolish the wreck with gunpowder. Their equipment was new and so was the work they were to do. They had to find out everything for themselves; how to use the new 'closed' diving helmet and dress, how to move about in the wreck without fouling their air-pipes and how to adapt themselves to working at a depth of sixty-five feet. It was all pioneer work which needed both intelligence and courage.

The divers worked in pairs, so that if one got into difficulties his companion was there to help. The guns, timbers, and fittings were sent up in rope slings. Among the relics of the fifty-seven year old wreck were the admiral's sword, a dog collar and a guinea.

When the salvage was finished they destroyed the hulk with oak barrels filled with gunpowder, exploded by an electric battery on the salvage ship.

It was six years before the wreck of the Royal George was finally cleared. The brave and cheerful team of soldiers did more than clear the wreck. They proved the efficiency of the new 'closed' diving helmet, found out how to use it and worked out for themselves the methods and technique of undersea salvage. Neither the helmet nor the methods have been changed except in detail ever since.

Divers at work on the Royal George

The Diving Bell

A diving bell is a strong steel construction open at the bottom under which men can work on the sea-bed in ordinary clothes with plenty of air to breathe. It works on the same principle that the water-spider uses. This creature spins a thimble-shaped bell on the bottom of a pond and then takes down air caught in its hairs. It releases bubble after bubble until the water in the bell is expelled and air has taken its place. When the bell is full of air the spider lays her eggs inside and hatches her young.

In the same way a diving bell is filled with air, which keeps the water out so that men can breathe and remain dry while working under water.

Some diving bells have an air-lock, a shaft attached to the roof of the bell. A man enters this shaft by an air-tight door which he closes after him. He then opens a valve and compressed air enters the shaft from the bell until the pressure becomes the same in bell and air-lock. He then opens the lower door into the working chamber, and closes it after him.

Diving bells are fitted with powerful electric lights and a telephone to the surface. They are used for work such as repairing lock gates and docks, for placing hawsers under sunken ships so that they can be raised, and dis-entangling wire-rope from ships' propellers and similar jobs.

Inside a diving bell

Diver's Dress

The diver's suit, like every part of his equipment, is specially designed with the knowledge gained by many years of research. It consists of layers of a material called twill made with pure rubber in between, so that it is watertight and airtight. The whole body is covered except the hands and neck. The sleeves have watertight cuffs.

A diver needs considerable weight, so his boots are made with lead and weigh thirty-two pounds, and a further forty pounds is carried in weights worn on chest and back.

The corselet is put over the diver's head and fastened to the suit with a watertight joint. This is a bronze covering for shoulders and chest, made to receive the helmet.

The heavy copper helmet is bolted to the corselet. It has three thick plate-glass windows, and the one in front, the 'face glass' can be opened. There is an inlet valve and an outlet valve, with which the diver can regulate the supply of air to his dress. Fixed to the helmet is the air-pipe and a telephone cable, with which he can talk to the people on the surface.

When all is secure, the air pump working and outlet valve tested, the diver goes into the water, usually down a short ladder. When he is submerged he gets hold of the 'shot-rope'. This is a rope with a heavy weight at the end which goes down to the bottom of the sea. Holding the shot-rope the diver goes down into the strange world of the deep.

Diving dress and equipment

Going Down

The diver must not go down the shot-rope too fast. Every thirty-three feet down, the pressure of the water increases by fifteen pounds per square inch, and air must be pumped into his helmet and suit so that the pressure is increased to equal the pressure of the water.

The diver is connected to the ship by the air-pipe and the life-line, a strong rope fastened round his waist. The life-line is used for making signals between diver and ship, or if necessary, for hauling the diver up. There is a code of signals; here are some:

Pulls on life-line	*Pulls on air-pipe*
One —'I am all right'	One —'Less air'
Two —'Send me a slate'	Two —'More air'
Three—'Send me a rope'	Three—'Take up slack pipe'
Four —'I am coming up'	Four —'Haul me up'

The call for a slate is so that a diver can write a message. When a telephone is used the cable is contained in a 'breast-rope', with a terminal in the helmet.

When the diver reaches the bottom of the shot-rope he finds a light line attached to it. He loops the free end over his wrist so that when he finishes his work he can find his way back to the shot-rope in the darkness at the bottom of the sea.

A diver about to start work

The Diver at Work

A diver's time is valuable. His task must be known before he goes down and he must work swiftly and carefully. The shot-rope is lowered as near his work as possible and the tools he will need are lowered beside him.

Just as diving equipment has been perfected by years of study and research, so have special tools been developed for use underwater. A diver can cut through steel plates in a sunken ship with a hydrogen-oxygen cutter; he can patch a hole with a gun which forces bolts through steel plating, or he can bore holes with a pneumatic drill. There is a special tool for every task. Divers also fix explosive charges which are fired electrically from the ship when they are safely out of the way.

Deep down the light is dim and sometimes it is made worse by mud or sand. To overcome this, powerful electric lamps are lowered which the diver hangs over his work. Sometimes he carries a powerful torch, sometimes a lamp is fitted to his diving suit or helmet. When it is necessary to crawl inside a wreck, the diver has to be very careful to see that his air-pipe is free, and that his life-line does not get fouled.

Two important pieces of equipment are an underwater watch and a sharp knife. The watch is to enable the diver to know how long he has been down. The knife is worn in a steel sheath at the belt. Most fish are harmless, even large ones, but there are exceptions, and then a diver needs his knife to save his life.

Working on a wreck

Return to the Surface

When a diver works at a depth of more than thirty-three feet, he has to take care how he returns to the surface. If he goes up too quickly from a deep dive the rapid lessening of the pressure on his body can cause very severe pain, paralysis or even death. So he must stop on the way up to allow his body to get used to the changing pressure.

The rests which must be taken depend on the depth and the time spent down, and they are all set out in special tables. For example, a diver who works thirty minutes at one hundred feet must rest, on his way up, for four minutes at thirty feet, eight minutes at twenty feet and thirteen minutes at ten feet, totalling twenty-five minutes in all. If he works for thirty minutes at a depth of two hundred feet he has to take seven rests totalling an hour and twenty-three minutes.

A special device called a decompression chamber is sometimes used. This is a steel cylinder with doors at top and bottom and, with a man inside, it is lowered beside the diver's shot-rope to the depth at which the diver has to take his first rest. Air is pumped into it so that the bottom door can be opened without the water coming in, and the man inside need not wear diving dress.

The diver enters through the bottom door, which is then closed, The pressure inside the cylinder is the same as in the diver's suit, so his helmet can be taken off. Then the cylinder is hauled aboard the ship, and the pressure in the cylinder is gradually lowered until it is safe for the diver to step out.

A diver climbs into a decompression chamber

Breathing Cylinders and Armour

Sometimes a diver carries cylinders of air on his back and dispenses with an air-pipe to a pump at the surface. He controls the amount of air he takes by a valve. The cylinders can contain compressed air, oxygen, or a mixture of oxygen and nitrogen most suitable to the depth at which the diver is working.

In some types of self-contained breathing apparatus, the air the diver breathes out passes through chemicals so that it is fit to be breathed in again.

Self-contained breathing apparatus is valuable for special kinds of work, as when divers have to go inside a sunken ship, when the air-pipe might get fouled.

The illustration, which looks rather like a man from outer space, is a modern kind of apparatus called diving armour. It is for use at great depths, where the water pressure would be too much for an ordinary diving suit. The armour is so strong that the diver is not affected by the pressure of the water, and can breathe air at the normal pressure of the atmosphere, as it is on the surface. The air comes from a self-contained supply within the armour, and it is purified to be used again. The designers' most difficult problem is to make the joints of arms and legs water-tight under very great pressure.

The diving armour in the picture is the invention of an Italian engineer, and it has been tested at the great depth of eight hundred and forty feet, where the pressure is three hundred and sixty-four pounds per square inch.

Diving armour—for work at great depths

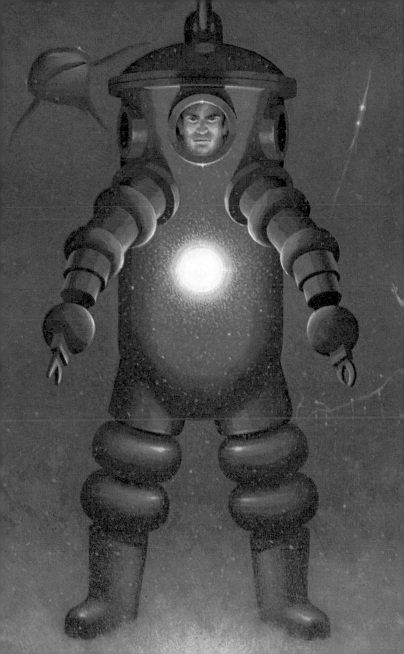

Submarines

A submarine is a warship which can be quickly submerged to approach an enemy unseen. It is made to submerge and rise to the surface again by using ballast tanks. They are almost empty when the vessel is on the surface and are filled with seawater to make it heavier when it submerges. To return to the surface the tanks are 'blown'—the water is blown out of them by compressed air.

There are other tanks inside the vessel, called 'trimming tanks', which can be filled as required to give the submarine the correct balance when submerged. Further control under water is obtained by using horizontal rudders at the sides, called hydroplanes. One pair is fitted forward and the other pair aft, near the propellers.

A conventional submarine—that is one not driven by nuclear power—has two methods of propulsion. On the surface it is driven by diesel engines, but as these need a large and continuous supply of air which cannot be supplied when it is submerged, electric motors are used, driven by power from large storage batteries.

The batteries have to be recharged fairly frequently by the diesel engines and the motors used as dynamos; so the submarine must come to the surface. This limits the time a conventional submarine can remain submerged, the longest time being normally thirty-six hours. The submarine shown in the picture would have a crew of six officers and about fifty-nine sailors, or ratings.

The general construction of a submarine

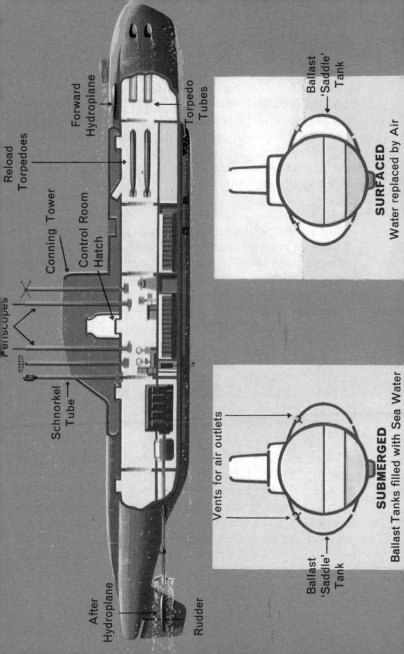

Periscopes

Conning Tower

Control Room Hatch

Schnorkel Tube

Reload Torpedoes

Forward Hydroplane

Torpedo Tubes

After Hydroplane

Rudder

SUBMERGED
Ballast Tanks filled with Sea Water

Ballast 'Saddle' Tank

Vents for air outlets

SURFACED
Water replaced by Air

Ballast 'Saddle' Tank

"Dive, Dive, Dive!"

A submarine can go as deep as the pressure of the water on her hull permits, if necessary to four or five hundred feet, but when it is going into the attack it remains at what is known as 'periscope depth'. The periscope is the submarine's 'eye'. It is a long brass tube, about forty feet long in large submarines, with lenses and mirrors and an eye-piece at the bottom. Through the eye-piece the same view is obtained as from the surface.

The periscope can be turned easily to see in any direction and it can be raised and lowered. With a forty foot periscope a submarine can be submerged to thirty-eight feet and still have two feet above the surface. In action, and to avoid the sharp eyes of an enemy look-out, the periscope is kept up for as short a time as possible and at the lowest possible height for good vision.

A submarine attacks other ships with torpedoes fired from torpedo tubes, which are right in the bows. A torpedo is itself a submarine missile, with explosive and fuse in the head, the rest containing the mechanism to drive it towards the target.

When a submarine is going to submerge the command given is, "DIVE, DIVE, DIVE!", and the klaxon horn is sounded. Things happen very quickly then. Every man hurries to his 'diving station'. The diesel engines are stopped and the electric motors started. The men on duty on the bridge go quickly below, the last to leave being the senior officer, who shuts the hatch and secures it with strong clips.

CRUISING ON SURFACE

DIVING— PERISCOPE NOT YET SUBMERGED

Ballast Tank full

Compressed Air

SURFACING

Schnorkel and Escape Chamber

The 'Schnorkel' is a device which has increased the range of submarines under the surface. It is a large hollow tube the same length as the periscope, through which air is sucked into the submarine when it is submerged. With this air supply the diesel engines can be run while the submarine is at periscope depth, which means that the batteries can be charged while the vessel is underwater. When the submarine is on the surface the schnorkel tube is folded back along the deck.

If a submarine has a mishap and cannot rise to the surface, the men can escape by means of an escape chamber, an invention of Sir Robert Davis, or through a compartment fitted with an escape hatch as shown in the illustration. Below this escape hatch is a cylindrical twill trunking which can be lowered into position. Water can be admitted into the compartment, compressing the air in the top of the compartment. Eventually pressure inside the compartment becomes equal to the sea pressure outside, and the water level then stops rising. The first man to escape begins to breath from the apparatus on his chest, enters the trunking, opens the hatch and rises to the surface. He is then followed by the others.

Escaping from a submarine

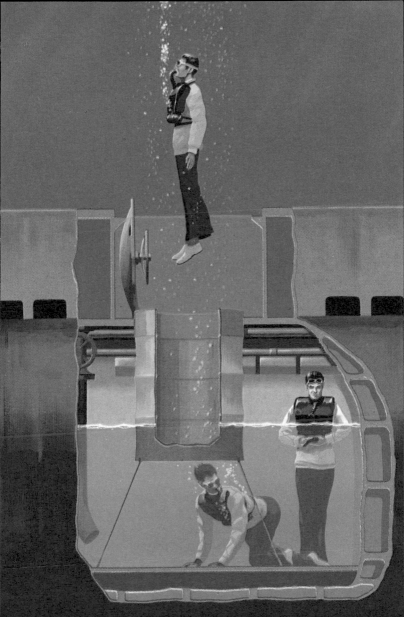

Midgets and Giants

In wartime, very small submarines are used to attack enemy ships at anchor. The pioneers of this were the Italians in 1941 and the British Navy took up the idea. Midget submarines take two or four for crew. The crew must be cool-headed, skilful and very brave, for their purpose is to penetrate enemy defences in the tiny submarines and attach explosives to the bottom of enemy ships.

The British 'X' craft used in World War II took part in daring operations. They were four-men submarines, two of the crew being divers who wore special equipment. They left the submarine by an escape chamber to cut a way through anti-submarine nets and then to fix magnetic mines to the enemy ships, returning to the submarine, through the escape hatch, when their tasks were done. Four men won the Victoria Cross for attacks in midget submarines in 1943 and 1945, and many brave men lost their lives.

In contrast to these midget vessels are the modern nuclear-powered submarines. When nuclear energy is used the range of a submarine is tremendously increased. This range is not limited to the size of the fuel tanks and just the one source of power is used on the surface or submerged.

Nuclear submarines are also fitted with air-purifiers so that they can stay under water for weeks on end. They have travelled thousands of miles submerged, including voyages underneath the ice of the North Polar ice-cap. They can stay submerged just as long as food, water and the endurance of the crew permits.

A giant, modern, nuclear-powered submarine

More Freedom for the Diver

The invention of the aqualung has given the diver a new freedom; he is as free as a fish. With no heavy diving suit to restrict his movements, and carrying his own air supply on his back, he can swim under water as he wishes. He can explore the underwater world at will, and take photographs and films of sea creatures and sea plants. He can go hunting with underwater gun or spear; the only restriction is the depth to which he can safely venture.

The diver wears a skin-tight rubber suit and 'frogs' feet' to help his swimming. He carries aluminium cylinders on his back which contain compressed air to last half an hour at a depth of sixty feet or twenty minutes at one hundred feet. Two tubes connect the cylinders to the mouth-piece, one for breathing in and the other for breathing out. A 'demand valve' on top of the cylinders controls the flow of air, but the amount he gets is automatically controlled to suit his needs.

A diving mask covers eyes and nose, a pressure gauge shows how much air there is in the cylinders and a depth gauge indicates his depth. He wears a special underwater wrist watch and carries a sheath knife in his belt.

Aqualungs are not only used for sport. Scientists use them to study fish and marine plants. Archaeologists wear them to examine sunken ships or drowned cities. They are used by men who make minor repairs to ships below the water-line, and they are worn by 'frogmen' who work under water.

Aqualung divers in action

Fish Friends and Foes

When a man swims with an aqualung he enters the fish world. Some fish are friendly, some curious, some indifferent but most are frightened and swim away. Only a few are dangerous, and because of them a diver carries a sharp knife.

Of the monsters, the whale is harmless because he only eats small fish, and the giant squid lives too deep to be met by free-divers. The octopus has a reputation for ferocity but in fact it is too frightened of a swimmer to harm him. Other fish which might be dangerous are conger eels, morays, sting rays, barracudas and, of course, sharks.

The friendliest fish are the porpoises, which like to play, and the seals, which are of course, mammals and have to go to the surface to breathe. Seals are highly intelligent as well as friendly.

Sharks are the most dangerous; often they ignore the deep swimmer, but one can never be sure. With their razor-sharp teeth, great strength and aggressive natures they are always a peril. They usually have an escort of small striped pilot-fish with a very small one swimming in front of the shark's nose.

Cousteau tells of a thrilling adventure in his wonderful book *The Silent World*. He and a companion had dived to inspect a wounded whale when they met an eight-foot shark with its pilot fish. For twenty minutes the two men swam in peril, while Cousteau filmed the shark, and even hit it on the nose with his camera, while his companion protected him with drawn dagger. Two more sharks, attracted by the blood of the whale, joined the man-hunt. The men had a very narrow escape indeed.

Danger approaches

Wrecks of 2,000 Years Ago

Modern diving methods have made it possible to examine the wrecks of ships which sank long ago. In the Mediterranean, ships of ancient Greece and Rome are found where they have lain for two thousand years and more.

Even when the ship itself has long rotted away, its size and shape can often be seen from the way the cargo is lying. When this happens careful measurements are made and underwater photographs taken before the cargo is disturbed. If the ship went down where the sea-bed was soft, the mud may have protected it to a certain extent. Mud can be removed by using powerful suction tubes.

Ancient ships often carried a cargo of amphoras, the large jars the ancients used for wine, oil or grain. Amphoras have been brought up with the corks still in place and the seals intact, bearing the trade-mark or name of the wine merchant. Empty amphoras are often used as convenient homes by octopuses and other creatures.

Sometimes parts of the anchors of ancient ships are found, and bronze and iron nails and other fittings. Ships have been found with a cargo of marble, beautifully made pillars and slabs which were being taken from the stone-mason's to the site where a temple was being built. Underwater archaeology is a new science and there is no doubt that many treasures wait to be discovered on the sea-bed.

Modern divers working on an ancient wreck

Sea Salvage

When the B.O.A.C. Comet air liner 'Yoke Peter' crashed into the sea off the coast of Italy in 1954, it was of the greatest importance to find what had gone wrong, for the aircraft was of the newest type. This necessitated collecting the wreckage for experts to examine, and as this was scattered in hundreds of fragments over four square miles of the sea bed at a depth of four hundred and eighty feet, the salvage problem was a difficult one.

All the latest methods of salvage were used. Asdic echo equipment probed the area, and when a contact was made with something on the sea-bed, an underwater television camera was sent down. This projected a picture from the bottom of the sea on to a screen in the salvage vessel. Often the picture showed that the contact was an old wrecked ship.

Divers could not be used in the ordinary way at four hundred and eighty feet but the latest type of observation chamber was lowered. In this a man could direct lifting operations by telephone to the surface. When parts of the aeroplane were found they were lifted in the jaws of a powerful grab. Trawlers and fishing boats dragged the area and brought up fragments, large and small, in their nets.

The search was long and difficult, but patience and perseverence were at last rewarded. After eight months work, in which nine-tenths of the wreckage was recovered, a section of the cabin top was brought up, and in that they found the fault which had caused the disaster. A salvage operation which had seemed impossible had been successfully carried out.

Modern science helps deep-sea salvage

Treasure of the Deep

Among the host of brave ships which have been lost at sea, many have taken rich treasure to the bottom, where it lies waiting for the venturesome man who can find it. Legend has it that a Spanish ship sank in Tobermoray Bay in Scotland in 1588 with gold, jewels and doubloons worth two million pounds. A number of attempts have been made to wrest this great fortune from the sea, but without success.

There are thrilling tales of deep-sea treasure hunts with modern diving equipment. Three famous ones are the salvaging of gold from the *Laurentic*, the *Niagara* and the *Egypt*. The *Laurentic* was sunk by German mines off the coast of Ireland in 1917 with five million pounds in gold bullion on board. The work of salvage lasted seven years at a depth of one hundred and thirty-two feet. The divers had to blast their way through tangled steel to the strong room under five decks, and crawl through small gaps. In the end all the gold, except one hundred thousand pounds worth, was saved.

The *Egypt* sank in the English Channel after a collision in 1922 and settled at a depth of four hundred feet. An observation chamber was lowered to direct the operation of a grab and more than a million pounds was salvaged in gold and silver.

The *Niagara* sank in more than four hundred feet of water off the coast of New Zealand in 1940 with two and a half million pounds in gold bars. The wreck lay heeled over seventy degrees. Again observation chamber and grab brought up all but a small fraction of the treasure. In one wreck, a diver had to go to the captain's cabin of the sunken ship, force a desk drawer and get the key of the bullion room.

Into the Deepest of the Deep

Divers and submarines are limited to a depth of a few hundred feet by the great pressure of the water. To go deeper something different is needed.

The pioneer of very deep diving was an American naturalist, Doctor William Beebe. He invented an immensely strong spherical observation chamber, called a bathysphere, in which he was lowered to a depth of more than three thousand feet.

The idea was further developed by a Belgian scientist, Professor Piccard, who had made an ascent of ten and a half miles in a balloon. Having risen to that immense height, Piccard turned his mind to exploring great depths. Beebe's bathysphere had been lowered on a cable; Piccard's 'bathyscaphe', or 'deep ship', was free moving. The spherical observation chamber, made of steel four inches thick with specially designed windows, was suspended from a boat-shaped tank filled with spirit. Weights were attached to the sphere by electromagnets, and could be released by a switch to ascend.

In his bathyscaphe Piccard went down to a depth of more than ten thousand feet, or nearly two miles. An even deeper descent was made by two French officers who went down in a bathyscaphe to a depth of thirteen thousand, three hundred and eighty-seven feet, or two and a half miles, where the pressure of the water was more than *two and a half tons* per square inch. The French bathyscaphe 'Archimede' has penetrated the Atlantic to a depth of seventeen thousand, seven hundred feet for seven hours.

In such vessels, equipped with powerful lights and cameras, man is beginning to explore the darkness of the unknown depths of the oceans.

A bathysphere descends into the unknown

The Diving Saucer

One of the scientists actively concerned with the development of the bathyscaphe was the famous French diving expert Captain Cousteau. Cousteau was a pioneer of aqualung diving; he has made brilliant underwater films and he has made important discoveries in his marine research ship *The Calypso*.

Captain Cousteau has designed a two-man, jet-propelled, research vessel which can cruise at a depth of a thousand feet. This 'Diving Saucer' is driven by two jets with movable nozzles, so that it can dive, rise, dip and turn as easily as a fish. Outside are fitted two cameras and a claw which can pick up anything required. Enough oxygen is carried to last two men twenty-four hours.

The diving saucer, and other similar vessels which will be built, can explore the bed of the ocean at depths far beyond the reach of any other diving device, except the bathyscaphe. The limitless wealth as yet untapped by man can be sought and used—the seaweed so valuable to the chemical industry, oil wells, deposits of chemicals such as sulphur, diamonds and much else.

The discovery of the Kingdom of the Deep has only just begun. Great progress is to be expected in the near future. Already Frenchmen have lived and slept in a bathyscaphe on the sea-bed. Perhaps one day there will be special kinds of farms under the sea. It is all new and exciting. This is called the Space Age; it is also the dawn of the Age of the Deep Sea.

A jet-propelled diving saucer

Series 601